For My Grandchild

From

Date

Grandmother

A Keepsake Book

Written by Barbara Briggs Morrow

www.debbiemumm.com

new seasons®

Artwork © Debbie Mumm

Written by Barbara Briggs Morrow

New Seasons is a registered trademark of Publications International, Ltd.

Louis Weber, CEO
Publications International, Ltd.
7373 North Cicero Avenue
Lincolnwood, Illinois 60712

www.pilbooks.com

Manufactured in China.

8 7 6 5 4 3 2 1

ISBN-13: 978-1-4127-5998-4
ISBN-10: 1-4127-5998-6

❀ Contents ❀

BEGINNINGS

For the Record

My full name is _____

I was born on this date at this time_____

This is where I was born _____

Here is a story my parents told me about my birth _____
_____

As a baby, according to the rest of the family, I was _____
_____

Place a baby photo here

My parents' names are _____

_____

These are my brothers, sisters, and other close family members _____

_____

_____

_____

_____

This is the story behind my name _____

_____

_____

_____

This is why I was given my name_____

_____

_____

_____

I was named after _____

_____

_____

My Childhood Home

Place a childhood photo here

I grew up in _____ and I lived there for_____ years.

Here is a description of my house and yard _____

_____

_____

This is what my childhood bedroom looked like _____

_____

Here is a description of the neighborhood where I grew up _____

_____

These were the shops and restaurants I loved to visit when I was little _____

_____

My Friends

My best friend growing up was _____

_____

Here is the story of how we met _____

_____

_____

_____

We most enjoyed playing these games _____

_____

_____

When I was growing up, the most popular game to play with friends was _____

_____

I am still in touch with these childhood friends _____

_____

_____

Here is a story my friends like to tell about me _____

_____

_____

_____

Our Pets

These were the pets I had while growing up _____

_____

Here are the stories behind my pets' names _____

_____

The funniest story I remember about one of my pets is _____

_____

As a child, I had these responsibilities when it came to our family pet _____

_____

Here is what I enjoyed doing with my pets _____

_____

Place a photo of the family pet here

Entertaining Memories

My parents enjoyed listening to this music _____

_____

My family and I watched these television shows _____

and listened to these radio programs _____

One of my favorite bedtime storybooks was _____.

It was about _____

_____

These were popular movies when I was a child _____

_____

_____

The top movie stars back then were _____

_____

It cost _____ to go to the movies.

When I was a child, this is what my family and I did for fun _____

_____

_____

Sign of the Times

When I was a teenager, if something was "cool," we said it was _____

The girls all wore _____

_____

_____

The boys all wore _____

_____

_____

The music I loved best was _____

_____

_____

My favorite dance was _____

_____

Movies that made a real impression on
me were _____

_____

_____

_____

Place a teenage photo here

Just Between Us

One of the hardest lessons I learned as a child was _____

_____

_____

_____

_____

My biggest struggle was _____

_____

_____

_____

_____

This is an incident that I still regret _____

_____

_____

_____

The moral of that story is _____

_____

_____

_____

_____

Wishes and Dreams

You might be surprised to know that I once dreamed of _____

_____

_____

_____

_____

_____

My dreams that came true include _____

_____

_____

_____

_____

_____

_____

As a young woman, if I were granted one wish, it would have been

_____

_____

_____

_____

_____

ABC's

The name of my elementary school was _____

It had _____ grades and _____ students.

This is how I got to school each morning _____
_____
_____
_____
_____

This is how children were disciplined when I was in grade school _____
_____
_____
_____

My favorite elementary schoolteacher was _____

This teacher was special because _____
_____
_____
_____

My favorite subject in elementary school was _____

My least favorite subject was _____

This is the type of student I was in elementary school _____
_____

Here is a description of how I dressed for school _____
_____

I started to get homework in this grade _____

Place a school photo here

My favorite games at recess were _____

_____

_____

_____

Beyond classroom studies, these were the school activities that I enjoyed most _____

_____

_____

_____

When I was in school, we did/did not have physical education. These were the games

we played _____

_____

_____

When I was in school, we did/did not have music and art education. This was my favorite

artistic activity _____

_____

_____

Here is a description of lunchtime at my school_____

_____

_____

_____

Reaching Higher

This was the name of my high school _____

There were _____ students in my graduating class

I got to school each day by _____

The high school teacher who most influenced me was _____

because _____

_____

My favorite subjects in high school were _____

_____

My least favorite subjects were _____

_____

When I was in high school, I had to take these classes that are no longer mandatory
today (like Home Ec or Shop) _____

_____

Beyond classroom studies, I was involved in these school activities _____

_____

This is how I normally dressed for school _____

_____

These were the cliques in my high school _____

_____

I did/did not participate in any high school sports. Some of the top sports at the school were

_____

I did/did not attend my high school prom. The prom's theme was _____

_____

Place a photo from a school dance here

After high school, I studied _____

_____

_____

_____

_____

The teacher who most influenced my life decisions was _____

because _____

_____

_____

The accomplishments I was very proud of _____

_____

_____

_____

_____

_____

_____

_____

_____

 _____

_____

_____

The one class that really opened my eyes and set the wheels in motion toward bigger

things was _____

_____

because _____

_____

_____

_____

_____

_____

This is something I learned that changed the way

I looked at the world_____

_____

_____

_____

_____

_____

_____

_____

_____

_____

_____

My Career

After high school, my career goals were _____
_____
_____
_____
_____
_____

My first career-related position was _____
_____
_____
_____

The best part of my first job was _____
_____
_____
_____

A difficulty I encountered early in my career was _____
_____
_____
_____
_____

Important skills that I developed during my career

_____

_____

_____

_____

_____

_____

I was excellent at this part of my job _____

_____

_____

_____

_____

I had to work very hard at this part of my career _____

_____

_____

_____

_____

When I first started working, here is what my work environment was like _____

_____

_____

_____

_____

_____

Here is how things have changed in my career since my first job _____

_____

_____

_____

_____

_____

If I could go back and choose any job under the sun,

I would choose_____

_____

_____

_____

_____

_____

I was working toward a career in this field _____

_____

_____

_____

Here is a description of my career path _____

_____

_____

_____

These are the accomplishments I was most proud of _____

_____

_____

_____

_____

_____

If I could give you one piece of advice about your career, it would be _____

_____

_____

_____

_____

_____

A NEW FAMILY

Love at First Sight

I'll never forget the day I met your grandfather _____

The first thing he said to me _____

My first impression of your grandfather was _____

_____

Your grandfather's first impression of me was _____

_____

We knew we were in love when _____

_____

Place a photo of the couple in love here

My pet name for your grandfather is _____

because _____

_____

Your grandfather's pet name for me is _____

because _____

_____

This is the story of our marriage proposal _____

_____

_____

_____

_____

_____

_____

_____

We celebrated our engagement by _____

_____

_____

_____

_____

_____

Happily Ever After

Our wedding date was _____

I wore _____

_____

Your grandfather wore _____

_____

My bridesmaids wore _____

_____

This is where we were married _____

_____

Place a wedding photo here

I will always remember this special moment from our ceremony _____

_____

_____

When I saw your grandfather at the end of the aisle _____

_____

_____

When your grandfather saw me coming down the aisle _____

_____

_____

These are the friends and family who attended _____

_____

_____

_____

Of the gifts we received, the most meaningful was

_____

_____

My fondest memory of my first year of marriage is

_____

_____

Becoming a Mother

Your _____ is my _____ child.

Birth date and time _____

Birth weight and length _____

This is a story about your _____'s birth

_____

_____

_____

_____

_____

Place a baby photo here

My first thought upon seeing my baby was _____

_____

_____

_____

_____

We named him/her _____ because _____

_____

_____

The first thing my parents said when they saw your _____ was

_____

_____

The first thing your grandfather's parents said was _____

_____

_____

Here are some details of that day that you may like to know _____

_____

To describe _____ as a baby in a few words _____

_____

The best part about being a parent was _____

_____

_____

_____

_____

_____

The most challenging thing about being a parent was_____

_____

_____

_____

_____

_____

As a parent, I worried about _____

_____

_____

_____

But I was really good at _____

_____

_____

_____

_____

Toddling Times

Here are a few of your _____'s firsts:

First foods _____

First steps _____

First words _____

Your _____'s favorite game was _____

The toy your _____ loved best was _____

Place a photo of the little one here

School Days

Your _____'s first school was _____

_____ also attended _____

_____

Your _____ had a real rapport with this teacher _____

_____

_____'s best subjects were _____

_____

_____'s least favorite subjects were _____

_____

This is the type of student your _____ was _____

_____

_____

Here is a description of how your _____

dressed for school _____

_____

_____

Beyond classroom studies, these were the school activities that your _____

enjoyed most _____

_____

_____

Your_____'s greatest triumph at school was probably _____

_____

_____

The school years your _____ seemed to enjoy the most were _____

_____

Place a school photo here

Telling Tales

As a child, your _____ got into trouble more than once because of

_____

_____

_____

_____

_____

The lesson was finally learned when _____

_____

_____

_____

_____

_____

_____

In our house, _____ was the disciplinarian.

Your _____

would say _____ was the softie.

Milestones

Your _____ gave me many wonderful moments.

Some of my proudest were _____

_____

_____

In school, your _____'s accomplishments included _____

_____

_____

In other areas of life, recognition came because of _____

_____

_____

Some of those honors included _____

_____

_____

Place a photo of the proud family here

AND THEN THERE WAS YOU

Another New Family

I knew your parents would be married when _____

_____

To me, their courtship seemed _____

_____

They were a perfect match because _____

_____

Their wedding could only be described as _____

_____

Place a wedding photo here

Becoming a Grandmother

When I heard you were on the way, I felt _____

_____

_____

_____

_____

I found out your mother was pregnant

when _____

_____

_____

_____

_____

I was so excited! This is what I was looking forward to most about becoming

a grandmother _____

_____

_____

_____

_____

Being a grandmother sounded like a _____ job to me.

I did offer your parents-to-be a few pieces of advice, such as _____

_____

_____

_____

_____

Waiting for you, your parents seemed _____

_____

_____

_____

Waiting for you, I was _____

_____

_____

_____

I couldn't wait for you to arrive so I could _____

_____

_____

_____

_____

_____

The Day You Were Born

I heard that it was time for your arrival from _____

The wait was _____

_____

This is how I passed the time waiting for you to arrive _____

_____

The day you were born, I _____

_____

Place a baby photo here

I saw you for the first time when _____

_____

_____

_____

_____

When you were born, you looked _____

_____

_____

_____

This is something special I noticed about you right away _____

_____

_____

_____

A special baby gift I gave you was_____

_____

_____

_____

_____

Candles and Cake

For your first birthday, I gave you _____

Your reaction was _____

Your first birthday party that I attended was _____

Your favorite part of the festivities seemed to be _____

The gift I had the most fun buying for you was_____

The gift I hope you'll always keep is _____

_____

Place a birthday photo here

Holiday Memories

All the holidays spent with you are precious, but my favorite memory is _____

_____

_____

_____

_____

The holiday tradition that is especially important to me is _____

_____

_____

_____

_____

_____

I hope you'll continue that tradition because _____

_____

_____

_____

This is a new tradition that we started because of you _____

_____

_____

_____

One holiday memory that I'll always remember is _____

_____

_____

_____

_____

One special holiday gift that I gave you was _____

_____

_____

_____

_____

This gift was special because _____

_____

_____

These are my favorite holiday dishes _____

_____

_____

_____

_____

Adventures Together

One of my favorite ways to spend time with you is _____

_____

_____

_____

_____

One trip we took together that I will always remember is

_____

_____

_____

_____

I could hardly keep up with you! You wore me out the time we _____

_____

_____

_____

Another time, I wore you out! Remember when_____

_____

_____

_____

_____

This is an adventure I experienced that I hope you will have in your lifetime _____

_____

_____

I think it's important for every child to have this experience _____

_____

_____

This is an adventure I am looking forward to sharing with you _____

_____

_____

Place a photo of the happy
grandmother and grandchild here

YOUR FAMILY TREE
My Branch

My family originally came from _____

_____

They worked as _____

_____

They came here because of _____

_____

Place a family photo here

The earliest ancestor(s) I know about is/are _____

_____

_____

_____

_____

_____

This is their story _____

_____

_____

_____

_____

_____

What I know about my ancestry I learned from _____

_____

_____

_____

_____

Your Grandfather's Branch

His family originally came from _____
_____
_____

They worked as _____
_____

They came here because of _____
_____
_____

Place a family photo here

The earliest ancestor(s) he knows about is/are

_____

_____

_____

_____

_____

_____

_____

This is their story _____

_____

_____

_____

_____

_____

_____

_____

_____

He learned what he know about his family tree from_____

_____

_____

_____

Traits and Ties

Certain physical traits run in our families. _____

_____

_____

_____

These are common traits on your grandfather's side_____

_____

These are common traits on my side _____

_____

Place a family photo here

In looks, you favor _____

_____

_____

In your personality, I see something of _____

_____

_____

You reminded me most of myself when _____

_____

_____

_____

_____

_____

_____

You reminded me most of your grandfather when _____

_____

_____

_____

_____

_____

_____

THEN AND NOW

In My Lifetime

Some of the things you take for granted were just dreams when I was young.

For example: When I was young, "fast food" was _____

_____

_____

_____

_____

_____

_____

My most "high-tech" toy was _____

_____

_____

_____

_____

_____

_____

_____

The height of luxury was _____

_____

_____

_____

_____

_____

_____

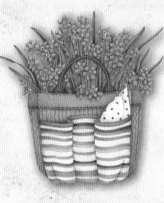

Some of the popular cars were _____

_____

_____

_____

_____

They differed from cars today in a number of ways, such as _____

_____

_____

_____

Not all inventions won immediate acceptance. Many people thought _____

_____

_____

_____ would never be a success.

Political Point of View

When I was born, the president was _____

The country's top concerns were _____

_____

_____

_____

_____

_____

_____

_____

_____

_____

These were all of the presidents who served during my lifetime _____

_____

_____

_____

_____

This is one significant international or national event that I remember from my childhood

_____

_____

_____

When I heard the news, I was _____

_____

_____

Place an important news clipping or photo here

I lived through this war when I was a child _____

_____

_____

This is how the war shaped my life _____

_____

_____

_____

_____

_____

_____

_____

_____

_____

_____

_____

_____

_____

_____

_____

_____

_____

In Perspective

In many ways, opportunities for all people have increased in my lifetime. For example:

_____

_____

_____

_____

_____

_____

Some of the most positive changes I have seen include _____

_____

_____

_____

_____

_____

_____

I'm particularly glad you live in a world where _____

_____

_____

_____

_____

_____

A LEGACY

Across Generations

The piece of advice that has served me well time and again is _____

_____

_____

_____

_____ gets credit for that bit of wisdom.

It was passed along when _____

_____

_____

_____

Years ago, when _____ said _____

_____, I should have listened.

On the other hand, the advice that I should have ignored

was _____

_____

_____

_____

Life's Lessons

One lesson life has taught me is _____

_____

_____

_____

_____

On the subject of love and marriage, I've come to believe _

_____

_____

_____

_____

_____

In regard to money and finances, I've learned that a good rule to live by is _____

_____

_____

_____

_____

Memories to Cherish

I hope you'll always cherish this memory of our time together _____
_____
_____

The memory of you that I'll always hold dear is _____
_____
_____

The character traits that I hope you will carry throughout your life are _____
_____

Place a photo of a special moment here

If there were only one thing I could teach you, it would be _____

_____

_____

_____

_____

_____

_____

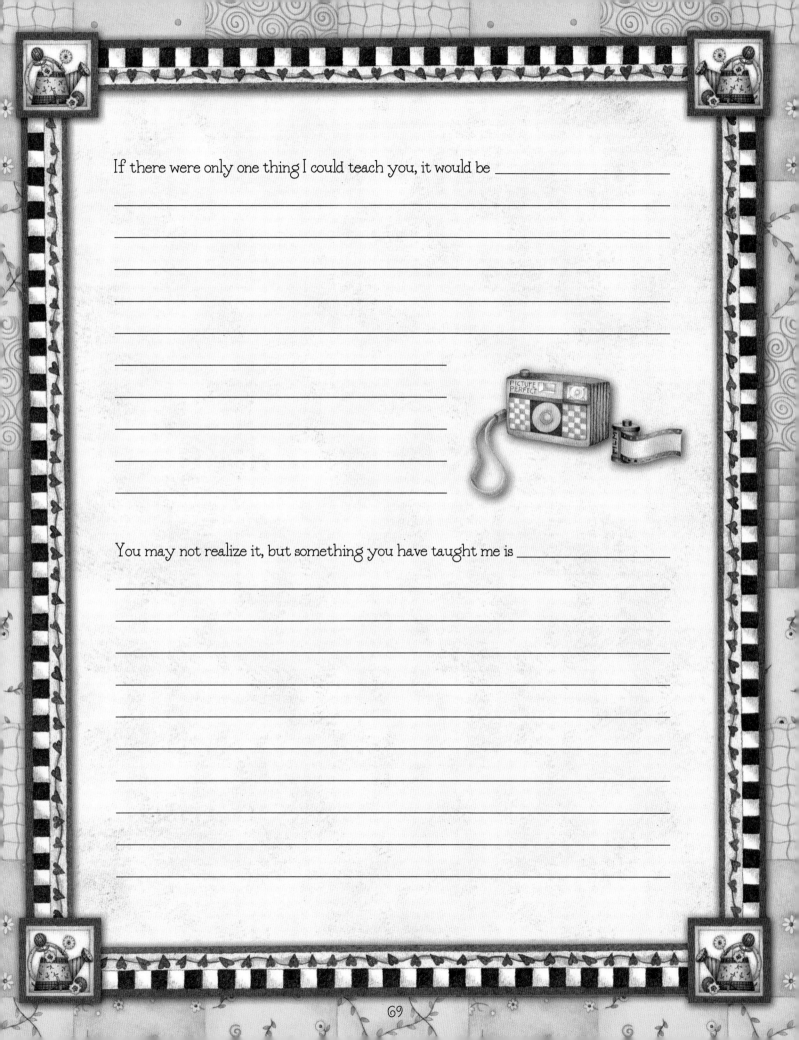

You may not realize it, but something you have taught me is _____

_____

_____

_____

_____

_____

_____

_____

_____

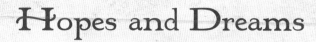

Hopes and Dreams

My dream for you is _____
_____
_____

From my point of view, it seems the best way to achieve that is _____
_____
_____

In difficult times, I hope you will remember_____
_____

Place a photo of an important moment here

A dream that recently came true is _____

_____

_____

_____

_____

_____

_____

_____

My most important values are _____

_____

_____

_____

This is an ideal that I still believe in very strongly _____

_____

_____

_____

This is an ideal I realized was not as important as I had thought _____

_____

_____

_____

_____

Place a photo of the whole family here

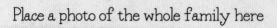

If I could live life all over again, this is what I would change

_____

_____

_____

_____

If I could live life all over again, this is one thing I would never change _____

_____

_____

_____

_____

If there is one thing to remember about life, it is this _____

_____

_____

_____

When you think of me, I hope you will remember_____

_____

 _____

_____

_____

_____

_____

Place a photo of the proud
grandmother and grandchild here

SPECIAL NOTES

Here is a place for you to write a special message to your grandchild. Use these pages to say something you've never said or perhaps do not say enough.

_____

_____

_____

_____

_____

_____

_____

_____

_____

_____

_____

_____

_____

_____